The Greatest Story

Written by: Pam Dixon

The Greatest Story

Copyright © 2024 Pam Dixon

grampamdixon@gmail.com

ISBN: 979-8-218-50639-1 (paperback)

Cover Art and Illustrations by Stephen Klink

All rights reserved. No part of this publication may be reproduced, store in a retrieval system, or transmitted in any form of by any means – electronic, mechanical, digital, photocopy, recording, or any other – except for brief quotations in printed reviews, without the prior permission of the publisher.

Printed in the United States of America.

Thanks to...
My Father God for being my Lord and loving me and all people so much that He sent His Son Jesus to save us, and for entrusting me to do this version of His greatest story. To Laura for listening to my ideas over and over and always giving me great advice. To Jenne for listening to this story from a pre-school director/teacher perspective and following up with great ideas. To Stephen for taking my ideas and thoughts on what I wanted the pictures to be and designing them on paper better than I could have imagined.

And thanks to you who are holding this book. I pray that God speaks to your heart of the great love He has for you and that you will share this story with others, old and young alike, so hopefully they can come to know the love of Jesus Christ for themselves.

In The Beginning...

Let me tell you a story of long, long ago.

You may think it's make-believe but that is not so.

It's the greatest story that ever was told.

If you hear it a hundred times it will never grow old...

God sat in the heavens with the Spirit and Son.
Three parts of God, all separate but one.
God said, I Am Love, that is just who I Am.
I need someone to love, and so He made man.

God put Adam and Eve in the Garden to live.
He said, all these animals a name you should give.
Eat all the fruit from all of the trees,
Just don't eat the tree in the middle. Leave it be!

God walked in the Garden and spent time with them.
It was all perfect, for there was no sin.
They cuddled with lions, the spiders didn't bite.
Everything was happy, not a tear was in sight.

Adam and Eve were happy and free.
 They ate lots of fruit but didn't touch 'the tree'.
They lived in the Garden; their life was not hard.
Because it was so easy they let down their guard.

The serpent showed up as bold as can be.
His sneaky ways were tricky to see.
He said you have all you could want, of that I can see,
Except you're forgetting the very best tree!

It's the tree in the middle so strong and so tall.
You can see it is lovely, the best tree of all.
Of that tree we can't eat. God we can't defy!
We can't eat from that tree, it we do we will die!

You will not surely die. Is that what God said?
You will not die, but you will gain knowledge instead.
You will be as wise as the God that you serve.
You'll become like a god, just as you deserve.

Eve looked at the fruit, it was luscious and red.
She bit it and gave some to Adam. Eat it, she said.
Then the serpent stood up so proud and so tall.
With a sly smile on his face he said, welcome to the fall!

Adam and Eve fell down to their knees.
What have we done? was their desperate plea.
With sin came destruction, disease, and despair.
The world was now wretched that once was so fair.

Weeds begin to grow, flowers started to die.
The world once so happy now started to cry.
A lion could no longer lay down with a lamb,
Fearing each other, they had to blame man.

God watched from heaven. He said, Jesus my Son!
Man needs a Savior, and you are the One!
You will grow up and live a life perfect in every way.
You will sacrifice your life to take their sins away.

Jesus said, Father, your will I will do.
He would come to earth as a baby, hope for me and for you.
Mary and Joseph, His parents would be.
The perfect plan of God they surely would see.

As the time drew near for Jesus to come,
Ceasar declared a census would be done.
To count all the Jewish people who used to be free,
So, Mary and Joseph traveled far on a donkey.

They went to Bethlehem to stay in an Inn,
But they were told there was no room for them.
Jesus was born in a stable where the sheep and cows lay.
Mary laid him in a manger that was filled with hay.

The angels sang in the sky as all of heaven knew,
God's plan for salvation was now coming true.
Sin and Father God can't share the same space,
But with Jesus's life He could save the whole race.

When sin entered into the garden that day,
It came upon all of the people to stay.
If you are a grownup, a child or a teen,
There's nothing you can do to on your own to be clean.

Only one who was perfect in every way,
Would be able to take our sins away.
Jesus was God, but He also was man.
With no sin in His life, He'd fulfill the plan.

Jesus grew every day and He never sinned.
He listened to his parents; He made them proud of Him.
He knew the job of His Father He must do,
He studied the scriptures, He prayed, and He grew.

He lived 33 years of His life with no sin,
Determined the plan of His Father to win.
When Satan would come and would tempt Him to sin,
He said, Get behind me! With the Word I will win!

Because Satan was evil, he couldn't understand,
The love that Father God had for all man.
The big and the small, the short and the tall,
Girls, boys, moms and dads, the Lord loves them all.

The plan of the Fathers is hard for us to see,
But sin had separated us from God and that's just the way it would be.
Unless someone could come and live a life free from sin.
Then they could pay the price and join us back to Him.

So, Satan put his plan into place.
When Jesus was dead, he could rule the whole place.
Men who were evil listened to him.
They arrested Jesus; they went along with Satan's plan.

They took Jesus to Pilot, the man to decide,
If a person is innocent or if they should die.
After he talked to Jesus, Pilot said, He is innocent of sin.
But the crowd yelled out loudly, crucify Him!

Jesus was sentenced to die on a cross.
With Jesus dead would mankind be lost?
They whipped Jesus' back, put a crown of thorns on His head,
He carried the cross as up the hill He was led.

They took nails that were long and had never been used,
They hammered those nails in his hands and in his feet too.
As He hung on that cross and His life flowed away,
His thoughts turned to you and to me on that day.

Jesus knew that the blood that He shed on that day
Would be what we needed to wash our sins away.
The plan is so simple, but we have to do our part.
We have to ask Jesus to come into our heart.

Jesus looked up and with his last breath,
He said, it is finished, as He closed His eyes in death.
The sky grew so dark, and the earth begin to shake.
All of creation felt a great earthquake.

The soldiers took Jesus body down from the cross,
And even some of them felt a great loss.
His body was laid in a tomb on that day,
And a very large stone was rolled in the way.

Sunday morning came and as the sun rose in the sky,
Mary headed to the tomb to have a good cry.
She saw an angel standing there and the stone was rolled away.
He said you won't find Jesus here! He is risen this day!

Mary hurried to the disciples, her story to tell.
She said Jesus is risen and all will be well!
Soon Jesus appeared, standing there with them.
They believed He was God's Son and bowed down before Him.

Now the disciples and everyone who lived after them,
Can receive Jesus as our Savior and live a life free from sin.
Free from sin and the death it would bring.
Free to live with God forever, forgiven for everything.

The payment of sin is death, that is what the scriptures say.
But where there is no sin then death cannot stay.
Only one who never sinned could pay the price for you and me,
Jesus lived a perfect life so His blood could set us free.

If you want to thank Jesus for all that He did,
Ask Him into your heart and then for Him you can live.
Just say Jesus, thank you for dying for me.
Now come into my heart and forever with me be.

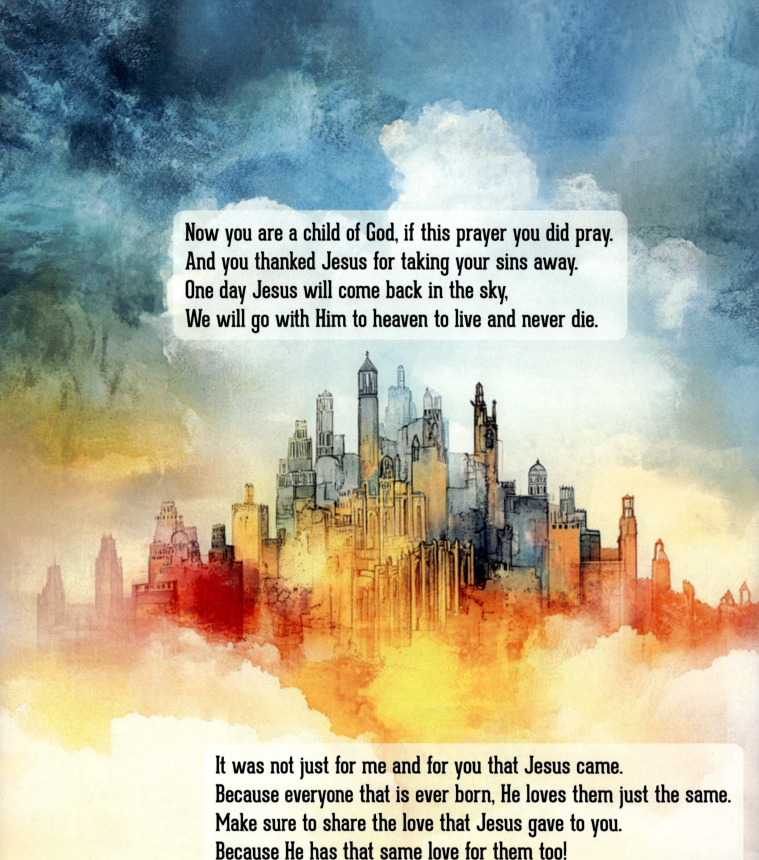

Now you are a child of God, if this prayer you did pray.
And you thanked Jesus for taking your sins away.
One day Jesus will come back in the sky,
We will go with Him to heaven to live and never die.

It was not just for me and for you that Jesus came.
Because everyone that is ever born, He loves them just the same.
Make sure to share the love that Jesus gave to you.
Because He has that same love for them too!

Made in the USA
Middletown, DE
23 October 2024

63182226R00020